D0603868

E.P.L. - WMC

Canada's
LAND & PEOPLE

SASKATCHEWAN

Heather Kissock

Weigl
CALGARY
www.weigl.com

Published by Weigl Educational Publishers Limited
6325 10 Street SE
Calgary, Alberta   T2H 2Z9

Website: www.weigl.com
Copyright ©2008 Weigl Educational Publishers Limited

Library and Archives Canada Cataloguing in Publication

Kissock, Heather
      Saskatchewan / Heather Kissock.

(Canada's land and people)
Includes index.
ISBN 978-1-55388-351-7 (bound)
ISBN 978-1-55388-352-4 (pbk.)

      1. Saskatchewan--Juvenile literature. I. Title. II. Series.
FC3511.2.K575 2007   j971.24   C2007-902209-X

Printed in the United States of America
1 2 3 4 5 6 7 8 9 0 11 10 09 08 07

We acknowledge the financial support of the Government of Canada through the Book Publishing Industry Development Program (BPIDP) for our publishing activities.

Photograph credits: Aboriginal Music & Arts Festival: page 15 middle left; Legislative Assembly of Saskatchewan: Page 4 bottom; Multicultural Choral Festival: page 15 middle right; Photo by Karl Rogalsky, Saskatoon: page 15 top; Copyright © 1995-2005, Royal Canadian Mint: page 4 middle; Saskatchewan Archives Board: page 13 top; Saskatchewan Roughriders: page 19 top; Saskatchewan Tourism: page 4 top right, 9 bottom right; Tunnels of Moose Jaw: page 17 middle right.

Project Coordinator
Heather C. Hudak

Design
Terry Paulhus

Contents

About Saskatchewan

Saskatchewan is the middle province of Canada's three **Prairie Provinces**. It covers 651,900 square kilometres of land. Saskatchewan became a province on September 1, 1905.

Saskatchewan is nicknamed "Canada's breadbasket" because it is the centre of the country's wheat industry. The province is also called the "Land of the Living Skies", probably for its spectacular sunsets or northern lights.

In 2005, Saskatchewan celebrated its 100th birthday. In its honour, the Royal Canadian Mint issued the Saskatchewan **Centennial** Coin.

Saskatchewan received its mace in 1906. A crown at the top of the mace represents the province's connection to the British monarchy. On the shaft, there is a thistle, a shamrock, and a rose. These represent Scotland, Ireland, and England. The mace was purchased from Ryrie Brothers, Jewellers, of Toronto for $340.00.

ABOUT THE FLAG

Saskatchewan's flag was adopted in 1969. Its top half is green and serves as a symbol of the province's forests. The bottom half is yellow. It stands for Saskatchewan's golden fields of grain. In the top left corner of the flag is the provincial shield of Saskatchewan. On the right side is the western red lily.

LEGEND

N

Yukon

Northwest Territories

Nunavut

British Columbia

Alberta

Manitoba

Saskatchewan

Ontario

Quebec

Newfoundland & Labrador

Prince Edward Island

New Brunswick

Nova Scotia

ACTION Draw your own tartan. On a sheet of white paper, make straight lines by dragging a pencil along the edge of a ruler. Make lines from the top of the paper to the bottom and from side to side. This will make squares. Use your favourite colours to fill in the squares.

Places to Visit in Saskatchewan

There are many places to see in Saskatchewan. This map shows just a few. What places do you think are special in Saskatchewan? Can you find where they would be on the map?

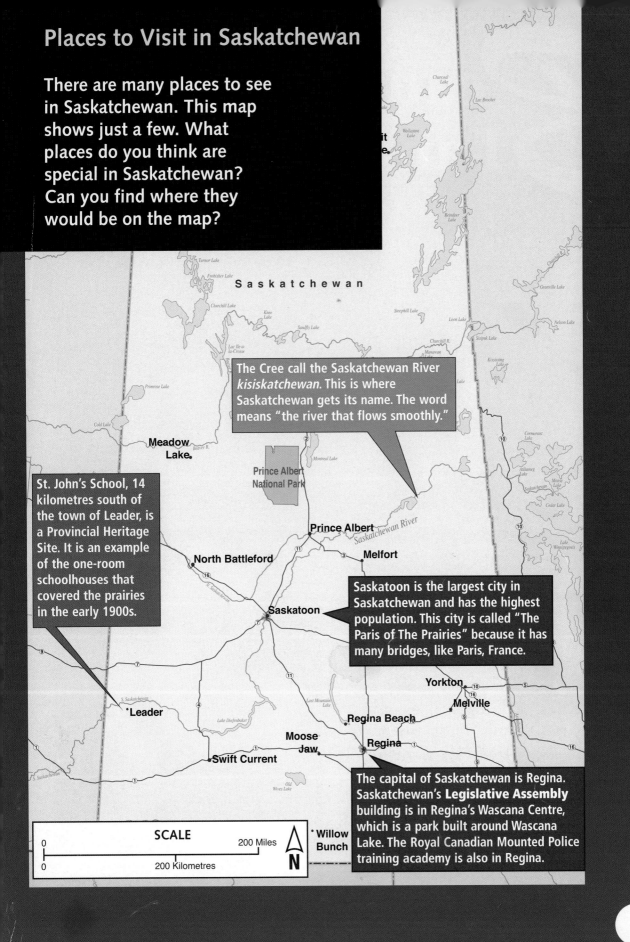

The Cree call the Saskatchewan River *kisiskatchewan*. This is where Saskatchewan gets its name. The word means "the river that flows smoothly."

St. John's School, 14 kilometres south of the town of Leader, is a Provincial Heritage Site. It is an example of the one-room schoolhouses that covered the prairies in the early 1900s.

Saskatoon is the largest city in Saskatchewan and has the highest population. This city is called "The Paris of The Prairies" because it has many bridges, like Paris, France.

The capital of Saskatchewan is Regina. Saskatchewan's **Legislative Assembly** building is in Regina's Wascana Centre, which is a park built around Wascana Lake. The Royal Canadian Mounted Police training academy is also in Regina.

SCALE

0   200 Miles

0   200 Kilometres

N

Beautiful Landscapes

Saskatchewan has many landscapes. The southern part of the province is known for its prairies, wide-open skies, and gently rolling hills. In the north are forests, rocky areas, lakes, rivers, and marshes. In many areas of the province are trees with bright-coloured leaves that shed in the fall. Saskatchewan also has two areas with high dunes of soft sand.

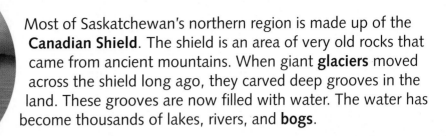

Most of Saskatchewan's northern region is made up of the **Canadian Shield**. The shield is an area of very old rocks that came from ancient mountains. When giant **glaciers** moved across the shield long ago, they carved deep grooves in the land. These grooves are now filled with water. The water has become thousands of lakes, rivers, and **bogs**.

South of the Canadian Shield is a boreal forest. The trees of this forest have cones and needles, not leaves. In this forest are woodpeckers, wood warblers, and flying squirrels.

Between the northern forests and the southern prairies is an area called the parklands. It features large stream and river valleys and groves of trees. The trees in this region include aspen, poplar, and birch. Moose, white-tailed deer, black bears, coyotes, pocket gophers, and squirrels live in this region.

The Interior Plains make up the southern part of the province. This region is mostly flat with some gently rolling hills, valleys, and grasslands. Many of Saskatchewan's farms are found on its flat southern plains, or prairies. Saskatchewan has more farmland than any other province.

Fur, Feathers, and Flowers

The white-tailed deer became Saskatchewan's provincial **mammal** in 2001. It lives throughout the province in wooded areas. Its coat is brown in the summer and grey in the winter. A white-tailed **fawn's** coat has hundreds of white spots. These spots disappear when the fawn is 3 to 4 months old. The adult male has large antlers that are shed in the winter. A new set grows in the summer. The white-tailed deer eats grasses, leaves, mushrooms, and berries. Its **predators** are the wolf, lynx, coyote, bobcat, and cougar.

Saskatchewan's provincial bird is the sharp-tailed grouse. It lives in the shrubs and grasslands of the province. This medium-sized bird has the nickname "prairie chicken." In the spring, the male birds stamp their feet and spread their wings to get the attention of the female birds. They also puff out purple air sacs on their necks.

The provincial tree of Saskatchewan is the white birch. This tree is also called a "paper birch" because its bark is made of paper-thin layers. It grows in cool weather and moist soil. Wood from the white birch is used for fuel, lumber, plywood, and **veneer**.

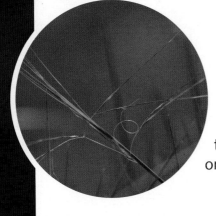

Needle-and-thread grass became Saskatchewan's official grass in 2001. This type of grass has sharp, pointed seeds. A blade of it looks like a threaded needle. It is common on Saskatchewan's prairies.

In 1941, the western red lily was named Saskatchewan's provincial flower. It was put on Saskatchewan's official flag in 1969. The western red lily grows throughout most of Saskatchewan and blooms from late June to mid July. Thousands of western red lilies covered the Prairies when the first pioneers came to the area. Today, picking the lily is not allowed.

Rich in Resources

Saskatchewan is rich in many resources, such as petroleum, minerals, and farmland. Much of Saskatchewan is used for farming because its rich soil is good for growing crops. Saskatchewan's farm products include grains and cattle. Almost half of Canada's grain is grown in this province. Wheat is Saskatchewan's most commonly grown grain. Other grains grown here include canola, flax, rye, oats, canary seed, and barley.

Saskatchewan produces about one-fourth of the world's potash. Potash is a reddish-brown **mineral** that is high in **potassium** and salt. It is used to make fertilizer, or plant food. The salt taken from potash is used as table salt and for de-icing roads. Potash is more than 1,000 metres underground. In 1997, students of Saskatchewan chose potash to be their provincial mineral.

Saskatchewan is the second-largest oil producing province in Canada, after Alberta. Oil is a fuel that is used for car motors and heat.

Saskatchewan is the world's largest producer and **exporter** of uranium. Uranium is a very heavy metal used to make electricity. Saskatchewan has uranium mines at Rabbit Lake and Key Lake in the northwest corner of the province. The uranium is sold to fuel power plants in Canada, the United States, Europe, and the Far East. All of the uranium produced in Canada comes from Saskatchewan.

Sodium sulphate is produced in Saskatchewan. Sodium sulphate is a type of salt that is used to make glass, paper, detergent, dyes, and medicines. Saskatchewan's sodium sulphate comes from lakes in the southern part of the province. Saskatchewan is the fifth-largest producer of sodium sulphate in the world.

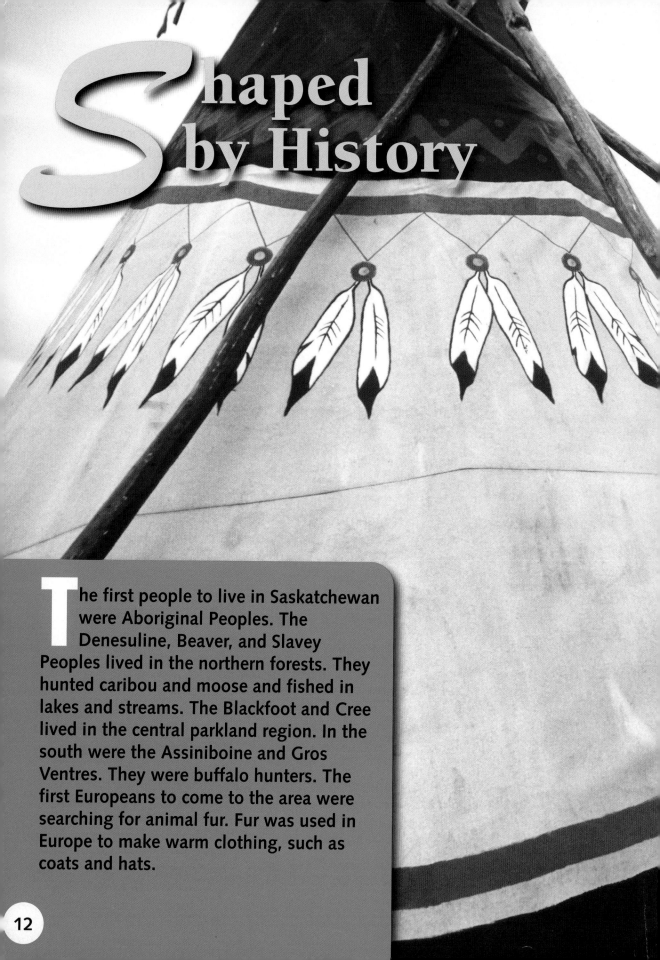

Shaped by History

The first people to live in Saskatchewan were Aboriginal Peoples. The Denesuline, Beaver, and Slavey Peoples lived in the northern forests. They hunted caribou and moose and fished in lakes and streams. The Blackfoot and Cree lived in the central parkland region. In the south were the Assiniboine and Gros Ventres. They were buffalo hunters. The first Europeans to come to the area were searching for animal fur. Fur was used in Europe to make warm clothing, such as coats and hats.

The first European to visit what is now Saskatchewan was Henry Kelsey. He was an employee for the British fur-trading company called the Hudson's Bay Company. Hudson arrived in 1690. He travelled up the Saskatchewan River to trade with Aboriginal Peoples.

Samuel Hearne built the first European settlement in Saskatchewan in 1774. This was called Cumberland House. Cumberland House was built in northeastern Saskatchewan, on the Saskatchewan River. It served as a fur-trading post for the Hudson's Bay Company. Cumberland House is now known as the oldest community in Saskatchewan.

In the late 1850s and early 1860s, John Palliser explored the prairie region of the province. He charted the boundary between Canada and the United States, from Lake Superior to the coast of the Pacific Ocean. He also looked for farmland. Palliser gave his findings to the British Parliament.

When the Canadian Pacific Railway was built in the early 1880s, many settlers came to Saskatchewan. At this time, the Canadian government gave free land to settlers.

Art and Culture

Saskatchewan is home to cultures from many parts of the world. These cultures include traditions from Europeans, Asians, and Aboriginal Peoples. Saskatchewan celebrates its cultures with festivals and events, such as *Mosaic*. Mosaic is a three-day event. It is held each June throughout the city of Regina. The festival features cultural foods, arts and crafts, singing, and dancing.

The city of Saskatoon hosts a multicultural event each year called Folkfest. Folkfest is a three-day festival. It features ethnic pavilions throughout the city. The pavilions have cultural displays, such as dancing, singing, food, skits, and storytelling.

There are many languages spoken in Saskatchewan. To honour these languages, Saskatchewan holds a celebration called The Annual Multicultural Choral Festival. This festival has been held in Regina and Saskatoon. It features groups of people singing in many different languages, including Chinese, German, Hindi, and Ukrainian.

Each year, the city of Prince Albert holds The Aboriginal Music & Arts Festival. This festival displays Aboriginal artwork, music, performing arts, and a major international **powwow**.

Saskatoon hosts a Shakespeare festival each summer. This festival is called Shakespeare on the Saskatchewan. It is held on the Saskatchewan River in brightly coloured tents. This festival has been held since 1988. During this event, the festival's actors perform plays written by William Shakespeare. Shakespeare was a British writer who died in 1616. He wrote plays and poetry. His plays are known throughout the world.

Points of Interest

Saskatchewan has many places to visit. There are parks, museums, an underground tunnel system, and giant sand dunes. A commonly visited place is the Wanuskewin Heritage Park. This park shows the history of Aboriginal Peoples from the northern plains. Here, tour guides teach people how the bison were once hunted. They teach how to build teepees and make traditional foods. Tour guides tell Aboriginal stories, dance, and sing.

Saskatchewan has a group of four museums called The Saskatchewan Western Development Museum. One of these museums is in Saskatoon. It displays a town from the year 1910. Another museum is in Moose Jaw. It shows the different vehicles used throughout history. The town of North Battleford is home to the Heritage Farm and Village, showing life on a farm or village in the 1920s. The Story of People Museum, in Yorkton, shows what life was like for early Saskatchewan settlers.

The city of Moose Jaw has tunnels running underneath it. The tunnels are now part of two different tours. One of the tours is called The Passage to Fortune. It tells the story of some early Chinese immigrants who lived in the tunnels. The other tour is called The Chicago Connection. It shows how Chicago gangster Al Capone and other gangsters used the tunnels for illegal activities.

Saskatchewan has two national parks. One is the Grasslands National Park. About 6,000 people come here each year for hiking and birdwatching. They also come to see Canada's only black-tailed prairie dog colonies and other rare and **endangered** animals. Many people also visit the Prince Albert National Park, which is in the central part of the province.

The most northerly sand dunes in the world are at the Athabasca Sand Dunes Provincial Wilderness Park. This park is in the northwest part of Saskatchewan. It can only be reached by boat or plane. Some of the sand dunes are up to 30 metres high and 1 kilometres long. According to Aboriginal Peoples, the sand dunes were created by a giant beaver.

Sports and Activities

There are many sports and activities to enjoy in Saskatchewan. Winter sports include cross-country skiing, snowmobiling, and bobsledding. Other common sports are golf, soccer, rugby, tennis, rock climbing, martial arts, sailing, and scuba diving. Saskatchewan sends many players to the National Hockey League (NHL) and has many junior hockey teams. Saskatchewan also has a rich history of curling. Many cities have curling clubs. In 2001, curling was adopted as the official sport of Saskatchewan.

The Saskatchewan Roughriders are Saskatchewan's only Canadian Football League (CFL) team. The team's home field is Mosaic Stadium at Taylor Field, in Regina. The team has won the Grey Cup twice. The Roughriders' colours are green and white. Some fans wear hollowed-out watermelon halves as hats at games.

Saskatchewan has five teams in the Western Hockey League. Saskatchewan also has 12 teams in the Saskatchewan Junior Hockey League. The Regina Pats are the oldest junior hockey team in Canada. This team began in 1917 and has won three Memorial Cups.

Rodeos are common on the Prairie Provinces. Saskatchewan holds many rodeos. Rodeo competitions include bareback riding and steer wrestling.

Many people in Saskatchewan like to fish. There are many fish in Saskatchewan's 94,000 lakes. These fish include walleye, perch, trout, Arctic grayling, goldeye, burbot, whitefish, and sturgeon.

What Others Are Saying

Many people have great things to say about Saskatchewan.

"Saskatchewan has a quiet stillness that invades your soul. The landscape is larger-than-life, the people down-to-earth, the cultural experiences authentic. There's room to breathe in our cities and towns, our beaches and resorts."

"See the northern lights dance above your head as you sit around the campfire sharing stories about the massive fish you caught that day. Take a small plane and fish your heart out on one of Saskatchewan's One Hundred Thousand Lakes."

"If you love nature, open spaces, and friendly people, this is the place to visit. Saskatchewanians (that is what we are called) are very friendly and always willing to lend a helping hand. The open spaces as well as the forests and lakes of the northern half of the province are perfect for those who need to get away from the crowded cities. One of the best reasons to visit, and completely free by the way, is the spectacular sunsets. Almost every town and city has something to see and do from museums to local festivals."

"More than 100,000 lakes and rivers make Saskatchewan a dream destination for world-class freshwater fishing. And the fish are something to write home about: 8 kilogram walleye, 31.7 kilogram lake trout and 137 centimetre northern pike have been landed here in the Canadian heartland."

ACTION Think about the place where you live. Come up with some words to describe your province, city, or community. Are there rolling hills and deep valleys? Can you see trees or lakes? What are some of the features of the land, people, and buildings that make your home special? Use these words to write a paragraph about the place where you live.

Test Your Knowledge

**What have you learned about Saskatchewan?
Try answering the following questions.**

1 What are Saskatchewan's two nicknames?

2 What is the capital of Saskatchewan?

3 What mineral is mined in Saskatchewan and used to make fertilizer?

4 Who was the first European to come to Saskatchewan? Visit your library, or use a computer to read more about this person and the history of Saskatchewan.

Make a Timeline

Draw a line across a piece of paper. Write important dates about Saskatchewan's history along the line. Below each date, write the name of the event related to each date. Look at "Shaped by History" on pages 12 and 13 for ideas.

Further Research

Books

To find out more about Saskatchewan and other Canadian provinces and territories, visit your local library. Most libraries have computers that connect to a database for researching information. If you input a key word, you will be provided with a list of books in the library that contain information on that topic. Non-fiction books are arranged numerically, using their call number. Fiction books are organized alphabetically by the author's last name.

Websites

The World Wide Web is a good source of information. Reliable websites usually include government sites, educational sites, and online encyclopedias. Visit the following sites to learn more about Saskatchewan.

Go to the Government of Saskatchewan's website to learn about the province's government, history, and climate.
www.gov.sk.ca

Visit Canada for Kids to learn more about Saskatchewan and see photos of special places.
www.kathimitchell.com/Canada

Check out A to Z Kids Stuff Canada, at
www.atozkidsstuff.com/canada
This website is loaded with activities and fun facts about all the Canadian provinces and territories. Scroll down to "Saskatchewan," and print colouring book pages.

Glossary

bogs: wet, spongy ground with rotting plants

Canadian Shield: a large, rocky area that covers much of Canada

centennial: the anniversary of something that happened 100 years ago

endangered: an animal in danger of disappearing from Earth

exporter: the person or group that sells goods to other places, such as other countries

fawn: a young deer

glaciers: huge chunks of ice that move slowly, usually down from mountaintops

Legislative Assembly: a group of people who make laws

mammal: a warm-blooded animal with hair that is nursed by its mother

mineral: a natural substance like a diamond or potash

potassium: a silver-white metallic element used in salts, fertilizers, and soaps

powwow: a gathering of Aboriginal Peoples who share news, stories, song, and dance

Prairie Provinces: Alberta, Saskatchewan, and Manitoba, known for their large, flat grasslands

predators: animals that hunt other animals for food

veneer: a thin layer of wood placed on the top of furniture

Index